Extrema Unctio
Satanic Last Rites

Contents

An Introduction to Agony

The book Extrema Unctio contains a satanic ritualistic text on dying. It is intended for the dying, for the already dead, but also for those who experience death during their lifetime. The text describes real human agony, but also the experience of the death of spiritual delusions and the rise to life in the glory of flesh and blood.

Extrema Unctio is a satanic book of passage, a ritual of the last anointing before ascending into the luciferic light, into the realm of undifferentiation.

However, before presenting the ritual itself, I would like, by way of introduction, to describe what dying is from a biological and psychological point of view and what symptoms accompany it. This will be helpful in understanding some parts of the rite of passage.

This introduction will therefore have to include some scientific terminology.

So what is dying?

According to scientific terminology, dying is the process of the gradual cessation of the body's vital functions and the build-up of necrophysical and renerochemical phenomena, leading to irreversible biological death.

Imminent death is preceded by an agonal state or agony.

This state covers the last few days and hours of the dying person's life.

Agony places the dying person on the borderline between life and death.

It is the period before the cessation of the body's vital functions, consisting of the gradual disappearance of vital activities. The agonal state is a process leading first to clinical death and then to biological death.

It is associated with circulatory and respiratory disorders and impaired functioning of the central nervous system.

If, during the successive stages of the agonal state, the functioning of the cardiovascular and respiratory systems remains at a minimum level, the phenomenon of so-called apparent death will then occur.

During agony, the functioning of individual systems and organs of the human organism is disrupted.

This process of dying, which precedes the arrival of death, takes place in several stages:

reduced life - is a state in which disorders of the functions of the central nervous system, circulatory system and respiratory system appear;

minimal life - is a state in which the dysfunction of the basic systems intensifies, leading to the disappearance of the manifestations of life;

apparent death - occurs after the state of minimal life and is an extension of it;

clinical death - or somatic death or relative death is manifested by the cessation of vital functions;

personal death - is associated with irreversible brain damage that results in permanent cessation of mental functions, regulatory functions and coordinating functions of the organism.

However, despite individual death, vital processes continue to occur in the body at the tissue and cellular level. The state of individual death lasts for several minutes. When vital processes cease, death occurs, which is a state of irreversible biological death associated with the appearance of the characteristic signs of death.

As vital functions gradually cease during the various stages of agony, this state is referred to as exhaustion of the organism, which prevents recovery of vital forces.

In people in agony, the signs of life disappear; however, it sometimes happens that just before death, the well-being of dying people improves significantly. This phase of agony called terminal agitation does not last long and is followed by the typical symptoms of impending death.

Symptoms of impending death:

progressive physical weakness,
sudden deterioration of health,
swallowing disorders,
respiratory distress,
drop in blood pressure,
increasing drowsiness,
premonitory rales,
disturbance of consciousness,

delirium,
visual hallucinations,
skin changes,
collapse of the eyeballs,
sharpening of facial features,
loss of sphincter control,
hypersensitivity to auditory, visual and tactile
stimuli.

Both the physical symptoms of death and the
psychological symptoms of death do not
always occur in every dying person. In some
people, agony only affects the last hours of life,
but it also happens that the slow process of
dying lasts several days and all the stages and
symptoms of agony can be distinguished.
Dying is a gradual process. It is a state in which
the body gives up on life.
In dying people, the body's systems begin to
act more slowly.
The heart beats slightly slower or with slightly
less force. Blood is therefore distributed more
slowly through the body.

This means that the brain and other organs receive less oxygen than they need and do not function as well.

Most people who die feel tired. They may sleep more often or longer. They may talk less.

As their stomach and digestive system slows down they may want to eat less.

The dying person may also lose weight and their skin will become thinner. Their body will find it difficult to regenerate skin cells in the way it did before.

A few days before death, the dying person begins to lose control of their breathing. She may breathe slower for a while and then faster, making her breathing quite unpredictable.

Fluid may start to build up in the lungs and the breathing may sound quite 'rough'. Coughing may occur.

In the days leading up to death, the colour of the skin often changes as blood circulation decreases. The skin becomes paler or greyer, and mottling or patches may appear on the skin.

The body temperature of people dying may change. Their hands, feet, fingers and toes may become cool to the touch. At other times they may be hot and sweaty.

With the loss of oxygen to the brain, individuals may become blurred and drowsy. Some people hallucinate and talk to people who are not there. They may become disoriented.

$\mathfrak{S}$ome people lose consciousness a few days before death.

In the 24 hours before death, the dying person sleeps most of the time. He may not be able to communicate when he wakes up because his senses are failing. However, he is probably still able to hear.

A few hours before death, most people fade as the blood supply to their body further decreases. They sleep a lot, their breathing becomes very irregular and their skin becomes cool to the touch.

Those who do not lose consciousness in the days before death usually do so in the hours before death.

Most people are very quiet during this time, although some may be restless or agitated.

$\mathfrak{S}$ome symptoms that a person may experience during this time include

glassy, watery eyes that may be half-open
cold hands
weak pulse
hallucinations
rapid sleep
wheezing or periods of complete respiratory arrest.

When someone dies, their heart stops and they stop breathing. Within minutes, the brain stops functioning and the skin begins to cool. At this point, the person dies.

Signs of death include

no breathing or heartbeat
the person cannot be woken up
the skin is pale and waxy
eyelids may be half open

the pupils are fixed
the mouth may be open

In the dying brain, structures that are not crucial for survival are first switched off. Instead, other areas of the brain, such as the visual cortex, become over-activated. This is why people in an agonal state often see flashes of light. This is confirmed by some cardiac arrest survivors. They speak of an extraordinary experience of another world that seems 'truer than reality'.

According to James Hallenbeck, a palliative care specialist at Stanford University, dying patients lose their physiological needs and senses in a specific order. First they stop feeling hunger and thirst. Then their speech is taken away. Finally, the sense of hearing and touch are 'switched off'.

According to James Hallenbeck, the subsequent stages of agony resemble something like sleep. Others compare it to a coma.

The above describes the process of biological death. But what might be going on in the brain of a dying person?

NDE

Some brain-dead patients who have been successfully resuscitated and brought back to life have reported experiencing a near-death experience (NDE).
In **Enhanced Interplay of Neuronal Coherence and Coupling in the Dying Human Brain,** published in **Frontiers in Aging Neuroscience**, this phenomenon is described as follows:
"Near-death experiences (NDEs) have been reported in situations where the brain goes into

a dying state. Subjective descriptions of this phenomenon are described as intense and surreal and include a panoramic view of life with memory recall, transcendental and out-of-body experiences with dreams, hallucinations and a meditative state. The neurophysiological signature of this phenomenon is unclear. It has been hypothesised that the brain may generate memory retrieval in this 'unconscious' phase with an increase in oscillatory activity. In healthy individuals, neuronal oscillations provide a temporal framework for the processing of perceptual, conscious and memory information during wakefulness, dreaming and meditation".

In the article **Brain activity in near-death experiencers during a meditative state written by Mario Beauregard, Jérôme Courtemanche and Vincent Paquette (2009)**, the authors write about this phenomenon as follows:

A 'near-death experience' (NDE) refers to an altered state of consciousness, usually occurring during an episode of unconsciousness resulting from a life-threatening condition (e.g. cardiac arrest, perioperative complications, intracerebral haemorrhage, septic or anaphylactic shock, near drowning or asphyxia, electrocution, suicide attempt). Typically, NDEs include a sense of detachment from the body (out-of-body experience), transcendence of space and time, tunnel vision, feelings of peace and bliss, and an encounter with a 'being of light' (often interpreted as a deity). Improvements in resuscitation techniques have significantly increased the frequency of NDEs. Recent studies indicate that near-death experiences (NDEs) are reported by 10-18% of cardiac arrest survivors."

The authors of this article decided to measure brain activity in people experiencing death in a meditative state. To this end, brain activity was measured in two separate experiments using functional magnetic resonance imaging (fMRI) and electroencephalography (EEG) during the meditation and control states. A group of near-death experiencers (NDErs) were selected for the study, who allegedly encountered a 'being of light' during their NDE. These NDErs claim that since their NDE they have been able to mentally visualise and emotionally connect with this 'being of light' during the meditative state.

The study found that: "The meditative state was accompanied by significant haemodynamic and neuroelectrical changes in various brain areas, including the temporal lobe.

$\mathfrak{T}$hese religious/spiritual/mystical (RSME) experiences can sometimes be triggered by stimulation of this brain structure.

Based on this finding, it has been proposed that RSMEs are triggered by transient electrical microeffects in this part of the brain."

The results indicated that the meditative state in NDErs was associated with marked haemodynamic and neuroelectrical changes in brain regions known to be involved in positive emotions, visual mental imagery, attention or spiritual experiences.

Interestingly, these changes show considerable similarity to those found in Carmelite nuns during another form of spiritual meditation.

In the publication **Enhanced Interplay of Neuronal Coherence and Coupling in the Dying Human Brain**, already cited above

The first case of measuring brain activity in a person who died during the study is described.

A continuous electroencephalographic (EEG) recording from a dying human brain, obtained from an 87-year-old patient undergoing cardiac arrest".

"Our data provide the first evidence from the dying human brain in non-experimental, real-world acute care clinical settings and support the idea that the human brain may have the capacity to generate coordinated activity during the near-death period."

This study, in addition to confirming that during the dying process, those brain areas and frequencies associated with, inter alia, memory recall and meditative states are active, also showed that the activity of the dying brain was similar to that of rodent brains on which experimental studies have been conducted "oscillatory activity in the gamma band was identified in the first 30 s after cardiac arrest (Borjigin et al., 2013; Li et al., 2015).

In addition to cardiac arrest, an increase in gamma oscillations was observed immediately after asphyxia and hypercapnia (Li et al., 2015; Martial et al., 2020)"

"the overall similarity of oscillatory changes between the highly controlled experimental rodent study and the present work suggests that the (human) brain may go through a series of stereotypical activity patterns during death".

In other words, this study has shown that near-death experiences (NDEs) may not only be experienced by humans.

It also confirms that the naked great ape, like other animals, belongs to the kingdom of flesh and blood.

The following satanic ritual describing the ritual process of dying is based on an unusual Tibetan ritual text entitled *Bar-do Thos-grol*, written by an anonymous author and dated to the 14th century.

Certain phenomena, experiences and visions presented in this old text are surprisingly consistent with recent scientific research treating phenomena such as the dying process and the experience by some people of the phenomenon of near-death experience (NDE), usually occurring during an episode of unconsciousness resulting from a life-threatening condition such as cardiac arrest. As I wrote about above.

This ritual text has an ambiguous meaning because, in addition to describing the experiences accompanying the actual transition from the state of life to death, it is also a description of a ritual of religious initiation during which the adept experiences a spiritual transfer to the land of death, a journey through it during which he experiences trials and frightening visions, and ultimately, through the understanding of godless reality, obtains a state of liberation and satanic enlightenment.

Here is the content of this rite:

Path Towards Voidness

Bowing down to all the fallen,
the Voidness,
Lucifer, who has descended,
to have all beings in his custody,
and to the ancient wrathful and indiscriminate
deities,
and to Mother Nature, perfect in her
indifference,
Bow down to the boundless, cold and dead
Abyss!

This ritual (method) of Satanic Liberation is mainly intended for Satanists familiar with the path of the mystery of godlessness, and it has a double meaning: as a method of the dying person's transition from life to death, and as a way of achieving a state of perfect Satanic godlessness.

First and foremost, it concerns the method of self-liberation of man from flesh and blood. One must first acquire the techniques with the help of which those satanists of the highest ability reliably achieve liberation by means of the transfer of consciousness. Should this prove impossible, one should practise this ritual of achieving Satanic liberation from the Circle of Delusion through Listening.

First the dying person himself should become aware of all the gradually appearing signs of dying. When they are all clear and unmistakable, he should perform self-liberation by transferring consciousness. If this is accomplished, it will be superfluous to read this Path Towards Voidness

If, however, the transfer of consciousness does not take place, the text of this Path Towards Voidness must be read loudly and clearly next to the body of the deceased. If the body is no longer there, sitting on the deceased's bed, one should speak with full conviction and invoke the deceased's spirit (visualisation) imagining that it is sitting opposite and listening.

Immediately afterwards, when the dying person has already stopped breathing, the ungodly person associated with him should read this text of the Path Towards Voidness to him, directly into his ear.

Path Towards Voidness

Sacrifice

It is necessary to visualise in the mind the object of the offering (what we are prepared to offer). Then the invocation of the fallen angels must be recited three times. Then one has to utter (preferably through glossolalia) a proclamation to the demons of the Guardians of Purgatory (the darkness of the subconscious), a request for removal from Purgatory and a request for access to the Abyss, after which one reads this text of the Guide to Death. It allows one to recognise three types of states of the Hereafter: The Light of the Moment of Death, the Insight of the Past and the Euphoria of the Knowledge of the Void.

𝕿eaching about the Luminosity of the Moment of Death.

Not everyone is able to recognise the Ultimate Luciferic Light. Therefore, reading this text to him is to help him recognise the Last Light and how to avoid stopping on the way to it.

Ideally, a satanist, whom he has asked for teachings, should be present with the deceased. If not him - then a godless person, an acquaintance of the deceased.
However, if none of these were present, then someone without fear should read the text in an unobjectionable voice. As a result, the subconscious of the deceased will recall the methods of how to recognise this clarity, and immediately, having recognised the Ultimate Luciferic Luminosity, will achieve the ultimate release.

Recitation time.

When the breath of the body ceases, the consciousness dissolves into the Last Knowledge, the luminous breath of consciousness appears. Then the subconscious awakens and appears on the paths of the hereafter in the form of phenomena; therefore, the recitation should be continued before the subconscious completes the visualisation. The time when the body has stopped breathing, but the consciousness has not yet dissolved, for the dying person stops, but externally it seems to pass more and more quickly.

Note: Ideally, the transfer of consciousness should take place a moment before the breathing stops. If, however, this does not succeed, the following words must be spoken:
"Son of man, who has now come to seek his way in the darkness! As soon as thou ceases to breathe, the Light of the Moment of Death

will appear before thee. Blessed are you if you recognise its meaning! And when the breathing of your body ceases, Consciousness will appear to you, unobvious and perfectly indifferent as the cosmos, bright, luminous, without end or beginning - pure mind. Recognise it then and step into the peace of its emptiness."

Before the body stops breathing, it is necessary to whisper these words several times into the ear of the deceased and imagine them entering his mind. "

Then instruction must be given.

This is the first state - the Light of the Moment of Death. The Luciferic Consciousness, free of any divine influence, is revealed to all beings.

At the time when the body stops breathing, but the mind - not yet, the consciousness dissolves into the Last Knowledge. People say that this is when consciousness is lost.

No one knows how long this lasts. It may depend on the state of the body, on the degree of understanding of the mystery of Godlessness and on the ability to meditate on death. It can last for several days. During this time, the dying person should be shown the Luminosity. During this time, the dying person may also sometimes return.

Attention. Ideally, the dying person should follow the above teachings himself. However, if he or she cannot, then let his or her co-participant in ungodliness, sit beside him or her and say:

"Now the earth is transformed into lava, lava into fire, fire into unconsciousness - unconsciousness into pure light".

These signs will appear gradually, and when they are revealed and there is a pause of breath, continue by whispering: "Son of man! Control your fear! Behold, eternity is coming, and thou art facing it. Therefore let thy thoughts be these:

Since eternity is coming, and I am facing it, towards it I fill my mind only with acceptance, compassion of fallen nature and indifference of the universe; may I, for the understanding of all suffering beings, attain the state of the Light-bearer! and may all that arises in my mind, especially my present thoughts, turn towards compassion for all beings cursed by delusional gods. May I recognise in the clarity of death the ultimate reality and in its sphere may I attain the ultimate Indifference (peace)! And if I have not attained it, may I recognise that the time has not yet come and that I may return. Meditating on the Ultimate Voidness, I wish to unite completely with all suffering beings, perfectly godless and free of divine delusions!"

Whispering these words clearly, directly into the dying person's ear, and not allowing him to be distracted even for a moment, one must watch diligently.

When the body has stopped breathing, one should say: "Son of man, here now appears to you the main, most important radiance; be willing to recognise it! Deign to observe it carefully!" "Son of man, listen to me! Behold, the Luciferian Light now appears before you. Recognise it! Son of Man, what you now perceive as a luminous void, devoid of shape, colour or matter - this luminous void, then, is your own mind, Luciferian Self-consciousness. And when, simultaneously with this one, a perfect darkness appears to you, born of nothing, pure, devouring light, expressive as nothingness, rippling as subconsciousness - know that this is Pure Mind - I Am. This mind of yours - luminous emptiness, devoid of substance, and a mind abiding in a state of jittery darkness - form a unity; darkness and emptiness abiding in a great sheaf of light, knowing neither birth nor death - this is the Light-Bearer. Recognising it is enough for your self-liberation.

When you recognise the luminosity of your own mind as Lucifer, then looking into your mind will be a contemplation of Lucifer."

This needs to be said three times.

First stage: a reminder of the earlier teachings of the mystery of godlessness, how to recognise. Second stage: the deceased independently recognises the luminosity of his own godless mind. Third stage: having recognised himself and having merged inseparably with Luciferian Self-consciousness, he reliably attains liberation.

By means of this method, the deceased having recognised the first light, gains liberation. But if the deceased does not recognise this first light - there will still be a reflection of the light; it will come after the cessation of respiration and the passing of the illusion of time. Then the unconscious of the deceased comes out and he no longer knows whether he has died or not.

He sees the figures of loved ones, relatives, he even hears crying and screaming. However, demons do not yet appear and the great fear of the Guardian of the Abyss has not yet arrived. Again, the instructions must be spoken: invocation and visualisation. As for invocations - call the deceased by name three times and utter the ways of recognising the light given above. In the case of visualisation, Lucifer's appearance should be described:

"Son of Man, meditate on your Mind! Focus your attention! Concentrate on Lucifer! Imagine his appearing form as devoid of independent being, as if a reflection of the moon in water! Do not regard him as a real form!"

Utter this in an emphatic voice:

"Meditate on the Lord of this World"

If, while alive, the deceased has understood the teachings of the mystery of the godlessness, but has not practised meditation on death and visualisation, he is not able to handle the transition on his own; then an experienced satanist or godless person has to lighten it up for him. But there are also those who were experts in magic (meditation), but at the time of death their illness took away their memory; to such unremembered people it is necessary to teach these teachings. There are also people who were once familiar with the meditation of Death, but who neglected the practice of magic; they are in danger of ending up in hell (the darkness of the subconscious), so these teachings are very necessary for them.

Ideally, the deceased should attain understanding at the first gate (first passage); if not - the satanic recitation will cause his subconscious to awaken at the second gate, and he will attain liberation.

At the level of the second gate, the subconscious of the passer not knowing whether he has died or not, suddenly awakens. This is the so-called 'Illusion'. Then, if the teaching is understood there, it meets the Void. Similarly, the light of a torch illuminates the darkness. Luciferian Light sweeps through the power of consciousness and liberation occurs. Thus the second gate appears on the path of consciousness, and understanding still depends, as before, on listening. If teaching then reaches the dying, the goal is reached. Demonic phantoms do not yet appear, so the deceased can go anywhere and everywhere.

Thus, if he does not yet recognise the Luciferian light, he will nevertheless recognise the reflection of the light at the level of the second gate and obtain passage (liberation).

If, on the other hand, he does not obtain self-liberation this time either, the level of the third gate, the Gate of Hell, will appear before him.

𝕯emonic phantoms will emerge from the third gate. Then it will be more important to read the Philosophy of the Gate of Hell; its power is mighty.

An experience of going beyond the body may then occur. The dying person then sees loved ones weeping, raising cries and lamentations, clambering around his deathbed. Although he sees them, they do not see him; he hears them speak to him, but they do not hear his voice. With an overwhelming sadness, he walks away.

Then there are sounds, glares and rays of light, and he faints from triple fear, terror and trepidation.

Then the Philosophy of the Gates of Hell should be read. Having called the deceased by name, clearly speak these words:

"Son of man, strain your senses one last time and listen with mortal attention! Existence has six states. The first: the state of bodily life, the second: the state of sleep, the third: the state of magic (meditation), the fourth: the state of dying, the fifth: the state of the Luminosity of Death and the sixth: the state of Emptiness.

Son of man, to thee have fallen three - the state of Dying, the State of the Luminosity of Death and the State of the Voidness; these will appear before thee.

Until now, the luminosity of the Voidness has appeared before you - in the State of Dying; you did not recognise it properly, so you had to wander in this state. Now two states visualise themselves before you: The luminosity of Death and the Luminosity of the Voidness. With all your strength try to remember my teaching!

Son of Man, now behold, you stand before the majesty of death. You depart from this world into eternity, as did all beings before and after you. You need no longer desire and long for this life. But if you lust after it and long for it, you will not be able to ascend into eternity; you will not yet be freed from the continual return to the eternal circle of life.

$\mathfrak{S}$on of Man, even if demons and dark phantoms confront you in this state of the Luminosity of Death, do not forget these teachings. Engrave these words in your mind and move on.

This is what recognition is all about.

"Behold, now the Luminosity of Death appears before me; I reject all wrathful, terrible and frightening phantoms and comprehend that what I see is my own visualisation; I also know that this is how this state manifests. At this moment, when danger has arisen on my path to my ultimate goal, I will not give in to the fear of a herd of angels, demons and phantoms!" - Saying these words in a firm and clear voice, understanding their meaning, go on. In this way you will not forget, the principle of recognising all phenomena as your own visualisations. Son of Man! The moment your body and subconscious separate, you will see pure Luminosity: its vision is initially small, brightly glowing.

ts radiance may make you feel uneasy. It will appear before you like a light in a tunnel. Do not be afraid of it, nor do you fear it! Understand that it is but the shape of your own Luminosity of Consciousness.

From the centre of this luminosity a mighty voice will come to you - like thunder, as powerful as the rumbling of a thousand lightning bolts at once, and it will booming loudly. But know and understand that it is the voice of your own Luminosity, and therefore do not be frightened by it! At the moment you only have an astral body composed of ingrained fears and subconscious beliefs, which is not corporeal. Therefore, these phenomena, sounds, glows and rays cannot do you any harm, they cannot kill you. You should recognise them as spectres arising within yourself. Remember the subconscious.

Son of man, if you are unable to recognise that these are your own visualisations, then, however much you may have practised magic in the mortal world, you cannot now understand these teachings; the light will frighten you, the sounds will frighten you, the rays will blind you. You will not understand the instructions, you will not recognise the corporeal nature of the trinity - the sounds, the light and the rays, and you will continue to remain in suspension.

Son of man! After a few days of vision in unconsciousness, you will leave here forever. But before that, at the very end of the path in the darkness, the last visions may appear, They are the lot of the few.

Time will reverse, as it were, and you will perceive all these delusions as luminous phantoms. The heavens will become like blood.

You will then see a vision:

A fierce wind from the east carried, A huge cloud shone, Fire burning and glowing all around, A gleam of polished bullion rising, In the centre four undead beings, similar to humans in appearance, Four faces, four wings, straight legs, hoof like a goat.

Bat-like wings, touching each other, Faces not turning, advancing straight ahead, Faces of goat, snake, dragon, dead man, terrible and savage, Circles on the ground beside each being, hoops high, eyes dead.

Between them coals scattered, like torches blazing, Lightning shooting from the fire, sparkling with brilliance, Alive but as if dead, running unnaturally back and forth, Five-pointed stars inside the wheels, hoops rising with them.

The wheels advancing as the undead creatures stepped forward, Rising into the air as they ascended, They walked where the spirit pointed, and the wheels danced with them,

The demonic spirit within them as they walked, also walked. As they stood, and they with them stood, And as they rose above the earth, the wheels ascended, Above them the vault shaped, glittering like splendid crystal, Stretched upward, over the heads of undead creatures sinister.

Beneath the vault, wings outspread, Mutually touching, creatures as if alive but as if dead, Two wings each had, the body shielding them, Advancing, a noise like great waters, like the groans of the suffering, like a battle cry, as they advanced, and stopped in place, A noise was heard from above the vault, their wings lowering, Above their heads something black, a tourmaline throne shaped, Man and beast, horns on their heads, holding a torch.

Above, something that resembled a corpse, a fiery glow all around

Then from among the fire one of the undead creatures turns its goat-like countenance towards you. Its body is of a cadaverous colour.

In its hand it holds a wheel with a kind of lightning inside. Because it resides in the fountain of subconsciousness, the corpse-blue light is the Wisdom of the Voidness, bright and indifferent, and this corpse-blue radiance radiates from it towards you, and is so strong that your eyes cannot bear it without suffering. Together with it a false light from the world of delusional gods will shine towards you - soft, white, dull. Then you, driven by the power of the false messiah, will feel great fear and trepidation before this truculent Wisdom of the Voidness, and you will throw yourself into flight. For this there will arise in your mind a fondness for this false light of white colour, dull. But thou shouldst not then fear the godless wisdom, clothed in the colour of corpse-black! Do not fear it, for it is the Light-Bearer of the luminous Wisdom of the Voidness. Full of the power of the will, worship it as a visualisation of your own mind!

$\mathfrak{I}$t is the Light-bearer Himself who comes forth to meet you in the antechamber of non-being. It is the light of Lucifer's compassion! Reject in yourself the fondness for the false dull white light, for religious illusions, for the hope of eternal life! For if you cling to them, you will henceforth wander in the realm of delusions meant for imaginary gods, and this will become a great obstacle on your path to liberation. Therefore, do not look at the false light, but bow to the truculent light. Concentrate on the visualisation of the Light-Bearer and say - repeating after me - this request:

"When thus, as a result of groundless faith,
I wander in the vestibule of non-being,
lead me, O Light-bearer,
on the clear path of godlessness!
I demand, lead me out of the still full of illusions and delusions vestibule of non-being!
Lead me through the light I now see to the end!"

$\mathfrak{H}$aving uttered this demand confidently and with great desire, the deceased in the form of luminous rays will dissolve into the eternal Void.

But if, even instructed, he feels fear of the corpse-like radiance (due to the action of the deceptive power of the instilled fear of an delusional god, guilt and despondency of nothingness) and flees, and if, in spite of having pronounced the demand, he follows the wrong path - then, after a short time, hosts of demons and a false messiah will come out to meet him, leading him to imaginary hells. And here is the teaching. One should call the deceased by name and utter these words:

"Son of man, listen carefully! Now there will appear a yellow, bright light of knowledge. And from among the fire one of the undead beings will turn his serpent face towards you.

From the serpentine face will shoot towards you a radiance which your eyes will not be able to bear without suffering. Together with it, a light will flow out, as if from below, from the area of the mind giving birth to visions of hell, the colour of smoke, next to this blaze of knowledge. At that moment, you will be overcome by anger and hatred of the godless knowledge. You will feel the fear of this yellow glow, and your mind will seek escape; you will cling tightly to the dull light from the hells of religious delusions, the colour of smoke. Then master the fear of the yellow bright light, understand and know that it is the indifference of Knowledge!

Bow before it and inspire confidence, for it is the brilliance of the Universe's indifference! Think then: "Here is my eternal refuge. The Ancient Serpent himself has come forth to meet thee in the tunnel. The light of the Serpent's knowledge is a razor for you, therefore worship it and no longer look at that infernal dull light of superstition, for it is a torturous path of reality-darkening lies accumulated by your childish beliefs. If you persist in clinging to them, you will fall into the abode of hell, into a swamp of unbearable torment; once you get stuck in it, you will never get out. That is why it is a great hindrance on the road to liberation. So do not look to it, give up blind faith and superstition, delusions and desires, but direct your worship towards the yellow light of Knowledge.

Utter these demands:

"When I thus wander suspended between worlds, thrown there by the desires of faith and hope, may you, Serpent, lead me along the luminous path of pure knowledge, like a mirror!
Deliver me from the infernal vestibule of non-being!
Enter me into the eternal realm of Ultimate Indifference!"

$\mathfrak{H}$aving uttered this request confidently and with great desire, the deceased in the form of luminous rays will dissolve into the eternal Void.

But even after this teaching some, as a result of false beliefs and contamination by religious delusions, will feel fear of the light of knowledge and will flee. Then it is necessary to call the deceased by name and speak to him with these words:

"Son of Man, listen carefully! Another day is coming, so the red light of the elemental underworld will appear before you. From the fire one of the undead creatures will turn his dragon face towards you. The dragon will appear from the abyss of the Underworld, in the red glow of the Wisdom of the Underworld, adorned with serpentine scales, and such will be its fire and its glow so bright that your sight cannot bear it.

From the face of the dragon will emerge a light that the human eye cannot withstand. At the same time, the pale blue dull light of superstition's hope will enter your mind. Then, through the power of the enchantment of religious myths, you will feel great fear and trepidation before this red glow and your mind will throw itself into flight; then a sentiment and longing for the pale blue dull light from the world of myths will be born in you. But do not be afraid of the red light! Recognise in it the Wisdom of Indifference! Enter the realm of indifference and eternal peace with complete serenity. Give it love! If you recognise in it the light of your own mind, you will already, without any further action, unite without distinction with all entities and teachings that have been, are and will ever be, and attain Luciferian enlightenment.

Look no more to that pale blue light from the world of myths, for it is a torment-filled path of accumulated religious teachings, superstitions and myths through your credulity. If it pleases you, you will depart to the Void in suffering. It will be the final obstacle to liberation, so don't look there and get rid of false hope. Get rid of ingrained beliefs! Do not cling to them! Give up hope! Worship the red dragon light! Speak these words of request:

"As I thus wander at the threshold of the Abyss Suspended there by the power of primal instinct, lead me, Dragon, along the red road of the Wisdom of Indifference!
Deliver me from the illusory hope of immortality!
Lead me into the eternal darkness that consumes light itself!"

After uttering this request confidently and with great desire, the deceased in the form of luminous rays will dissolve into eternal Darkness.

After such instructions, even a weak-willed person will undoubtedly experience a transformation. But if, even in the face of repeated instruction, he still now fails to recognise the path correctly; flushed by the power of religious passions and the taint of ungodly knowledge, he will feel fear of disturbing sounds and light, and will begin to flee.

The next day, however, a legion of the dead in faith will come out to meet him on the luminous road to Nothingness, hungry wraiths - created by the subconscious, arising from fear and envy.

The tip is this. The deceased should be called by name and addressed thus:

"Son of man, listen carefully! Another day has come, so that the bright light of the element of fire will appear before you. Then from the western sky, which will turn red, a fourth undead being will emerge.

$\mathfrak{I}$t will turn its disturbing goat's face towards you. From within it, a glow will emerge that will penetrate your heart. A glow so bright that no eye can bear it. But do not be afraid of it! When the pale, dull glow of superstition appears along with this radiance of godless wisdom, do not look upon it with kindness! Abandon your attachment to it!

Then, as a result of the powerful forces of beliefs and convictions rooted in the subconscious, you will feel fear before the bright light of the element of fire, and will throw yourself into flight. On the other hand, a desire and attachment to the dull glow of superstition will be born in you. At that moment you should, in that bright, fiery light, recognise the Godless Wisdom, and not be afraid of it. Immediately thereafter, in the calmness of indifference, enter the sphere of Godless Wisdom and bow down to it.

If you then recognise it for what it really is, that is, the light of your own godlessness, then without even bowing to it you will merge with all these undead beings and lights, and attain satanic enlightenment. If by all means you do not recognise it as such, then think then that it is the light of luciferic wisdom and your refuge. Bow down to it in your thoughts; it is the radiance of the enlightenment of the Son of Dawn. Do not flee from it! But even if you flee, you will still remain inseparable. Do not turn your face towards this dull light of superstition, for it is the path of pernicious delusions gathered by your subconscious. If it pleases you, you will roll down it into a hell of fear of the unknown and experience the hellish torments of fear and illusory hope. This is a great obstacle on the path to liberation, so do not attach yourself to it and abandon false inclinations! Do not attach yourself to them! Worship the light of fire, meditate on Lucifer and say these desires:

𝔚hile I am thus wandering in the circle of delusion, thrust into it by the superstitiously deluded subconscious, may you, O Demon with the Face of the Goat, guide me along the Fiery Path of the Light of Godless Wisdom! Liberate me from the hell of the interworlds! Lead me to the paradise of lost instincts!"

Having uttered this request with conviction and certainty, the deceased will experience the transition by dissolving into the primordial light. Acting in this way with conviction, one cannot fail to experience liberation. However, as a result of succumbing to the tendency to believe in the superstitions instilled during life and the ingrained fears of imaginary punishment, the deceased is unable to rid himself of them completely, so that the deluded subconscious and the envy of imaginary worlds will give rise to anger and fear of demonic sounds and fiery light, so that he will not grasp the grace of the peace of godlessness. Therefore, he will wander there, in a circle of delusion, until the next day.

On the next day, all four undead beings will appear to him simultaneously. Together, too, the five lights of the five spheres of the Eternal Void will shine forth.

Here is the teaching. One should call the deceased by name and say these words:

"Son of man, listen carefully! Until yesterday, four kinds of brightness appeared before you, consecutively. Contrary to the teachings given to you, the deceptive power of superstition and the evil of indoctrination caused you to be seized with blindness and fear; therefore, until yesterday, you wandered in a circle of delusion. If you had recognised these four types of radiance of the Godless Wisdom as your own visualisations, you would have dissolved into one of these lights and become one with the Luciferian light.

But since you have not recognised it, you are wandering in a circle of delusion. Watch carefully then!

Now the five figures of perfect light and the phantoms of the Four Infernal Wisdoms will come out to meet you. Recognise them! Son of man, behold, under the form of four fiery brightnesses, the four elements will appear to you. In the middle, from the area of the black sky of the Eternal Universe, Satan will appear. On the eastern side, from the red sky area of the Carnal Delight, the Serpent will appear. On the south side, from the white sky of Indifference, the Devil will appear. On the west side, from the golden sky area of Emotion, the Dragon will appear. On the northern side, from the silver sky area of Supreme Perfection, Lucifer will appear; he will emerge before you from the light of the stars.

Son of man, further on, behind these five figures, the gates are guarded by powerful demons:

The first Demon on a white horse with a scythe in his hand and a crown on his head, the second Demon on a fiery red horse with a sword in his hand, the third Demon on a black horse with a scale in his hand and the fourth Demon on a pale horse, and his name Death.

When the 13 old men wearing crowns with horns emerge from within your own mind, then - because they appear to you - recognise them as your own visualisation.

Son of man! All these realms and realms of heaven are not in any one place; in fact, they are the four sides of your own subconscious. Now these phantoms emerge from the greatest depths of your subconscious and appear to you. They do not emerge from any other place, therefore recognise in them the eternal deceptive play of your own mind.

Son of man! These phantoms will have their proper colours. They will be located on a five-pointed star, each surrounded by a halo of light.

These figures will appear all at once, as a virtual sigil. Recognise them as your guiding deity!

Son of man, from the minds of these five luminous demons there will crawl towards your subconsciousness, thin as a snake, bright and shining like a moonbeam, the silvery light of the four Infernal Wisdoms united: first the mind of Satan will be joined to yours by the black, light-absorbing, anxiety-inducing ray of the Knowledge of the Mystery of Ungodliness. Inside this peculiar fabric created by the fusion of minds, a white disc shines, very bright and luminous, emanating as if from the bottom of a mirror. It will appear surrounded by similar small discs and specks, with no centre or circumference.

From the mind of the Serpent will crawl the Sinful Knowledge of Flesh and Blood, red in colour, bright; red discs will be visible on its fabric.

From the mind of the Devil will crawl the bright white light of the Knowledge of Indiscrimination; its fabric is adorned with luminous discs.

From the mind of the Dragon will crawl the yellow bright light of the Wisdom of Unbridled Emotion; its fabric is adorned with red luminous discs. They will appear as having no circumference or centre.

Son of Man, they are all visualisations arising from the deceptive play of thy own mind; they have not originated from anything external. Do not desire them, nor fear them; calmly enter the realm of thought called the Indifference of the Void. There these demons and lights will dissolve in you and you will attain liberation.

The silver gleam of Ultimate Knowledge will not appear to thee, for the deceptive play of thy own wisdom has not yet been completed.

$\mathfrak{S}$on of man, they are all like the delusions of infernal Wisdom and constitute the path of Ungodliness. Then you must remind yourself of the teachings and instructions contained in the ungodly theology of the Mystery of Godlessness. If you recall their meaning, you will be filled with confidence in all these previously seen demonic phantoms, and it will be like meeting dead loved ones; you will recognise them when you see them, but as if in a mirror, and you will stop doubting. When you realise that these phantoms come from yourself - you will ascend the path towards the absorbing light of darkness, which gives ultimate freedom. As a result of the resulting conviction, complete absorption will be born in your mind, and having melted into the wisdom of the eternal like death and indifferent emptiness, you will become a reflection of Lucifer, so that you will no longer return to worldly life.

$\mathfrak{S}$on of man, together with the light of Godless Wisdom, six kinds of dim, deceptive radiance will dawn before you. The first, a white, spotless light from the world of delusional gods; the second, a red, spotless light from the hell of fear of eternal punishment; the third, a blue, spotless light from the area of delusional guilt; the fourth, a green, spotless light from the area of instilled shame; the fifth, a yellow, spotless light from the area of blind faith and ignorance; the sixth, an ashen, spotless light from the area of illusory hope. These will accompany those hellishly fiery lights of Godless Wisdom.

You must not then show any attachment to any of them; ascend in the calm of cold indifference into the sphere of consciousness without distinction.

If, however, you are frightened by the fiery light of the Mystery of Godlessness and attracted by the dim glow of the six areas of the wheel of delusion, your mind will then merge with one of the phenomena representing them and you will again wander in the darkness of fear and delusion until you completely lose the will to power.

Son of man, if you have not acquainted yourself with the path of the Mystery of Godlessness, in the face of all these phantoms and lights of Godless Knowledge you will feel fear and trepidation, and turn to the dull glow of the wheel of delusion; resolve not to do so, Turn then to those bright and fiery lights of Godless Wisdom. Think thus: "This is the light of the Mystery of Godlessness, the wisdom of the five Demons who have come to sustain me; they are my refuge." So, do not cling to these six deceptive lights and hold them in contempt, but focus with all your might on the five Devil figures and speak thus:

"When I thus wander in the wheel of delusion, thrown into it by six poisons,
I demand, O Satanic Emissaries, be my guides on the fiery path of the four Infernal Wisdoms!

eliver me from the deceptive path leading to the six terrible realms of the wheel of delusion!
Deliver me from the purgatory of unwillingness!
Guide me through the darkness that consumes the light!"

Having uttered this demand and realised that these phantoms are only his own visualisations, the deceased attains Luciferic Luminosity. If he is a conscious satanist, by the power of the wisdom of his instincts he will comprehend all this on his own and attain liberation. Even novice adepts, by the mere understanding of the nature of religious delusions, will achieve that the entrances to the areas of the delusional wheel will close before them, and through the contemplation of the infernal Wisdoms, they will attain enlightenment by following the path of the Mystery of Godlessness.

$\mathfrak{H}$aving thus attained indifference and recognised the true nature of things, many access eternal liberation. Ultimately, however, those who lack the will to power, even if they have received teachings and methods, are unable to recognise correctly as a result of having gone astray through the fault of the preachers of illusion, ignorance of the Mystery of Godlessness, being surrounded by the slaves of an imaginary god and misappropriation of the path of flesh and blood. Therefore, they will enter the circle of delusion and will wander in it for a long time.

On the last day, a crowd of fallen angels will emerge from the moonlight of the heavenly area of the Pure Void to meet the dying. At the same time, a clear path will appear leading to the area of the hell of delusion, created from the contamination of blind faith and ignorance. Then again, instruction must be given.

Call the dead man by name and speak to him thus:

"Son of man, listen carefully! On the last day the radiance of the sphere of divine fear and habits of faith will appear to you. From the moonlight of the expanse of the heavens of the Pure Voidness, fallen angels will come forth to meet you in crowds. In the middle of a sigil shrouded in silvery radiance will appear the Son of Dawn, the Utterly Perfect Light named Lucifer. His body shines with five radiance. Levitating, he holds a bloody sword and an angelic skull full of blood, makes hostile gestures and angrily looks up into the sky.

On the eastern side of the sigil, an Air Spirit with a body of white will appear. Levitating, he holds in his hands a bloody sword and a skull full of angelic blood, makes unfriendly gestures and angrily looks up at the sky.

$\mathcal{O}$n the southern side of the sigil, the Fire Spirit appears with a yellow body. Levitating, he holds in his hands a bloody sword and an angelic skull full of blood, makes mysterious gestures and stares angrily into the sky.

On the western side of the sigil, an Earth Spirit with a body of red will appear.
Levitating, he holds a bloody sword and a skull full of angelic blood, makes angry gestures and looks up to the sky with contempt.

On the north side of the sigil, the Water Spirit appears with a blue body and a face contorted in a grimace of anger. Levitating, he holds a scythe sword and a skull full of angelic blood, makes mysterious gestures and looks up to the sky with hatred.

These spirits will be accompanied by a gradual appearance of countless crowds of women witches - as well as kings and rulers and their retinues; in addition, various gods and goddesses and crowds of guardian gods, all clad in rich robes and ornaments made of bone. Accompanied by the music of drums, flutes made of pipes and horns, carrying turquoise pennants made of human skin, canopies and leather tassels, amid the smoke of frying human bodies and disturbing music, the whole crowd will fill all corners of the world with sensual rippling, rolling with foam on their lips, staggering from the intoxication of wine and shaking. Dancing and prancing in various ways, they step forward to meet - the ungodly to welcome him, the deceived to punish him.

Son of man, from the minds of these five fallen angels, a fiery and unpleasant glow, bright and thin, rippling, writhing and shimmering multicoloured thread of Godless Wisdom, born of its own accord in the sphere of unconscious inclinations and instincts, will emerge like a snake and enter your mind. It is fiery, shining so strongly and brightly that the eye cannot bear it. Along with it, next to it, there will appear a blue dull light coming from the realm of the imaginary paradise - together with the radiance of the Godless Wisdom. Then, as a result of the deceptive power of the desire to believe in delusions, a fear of this multicoloured light will arise in you, and you will begin to flee, and cling to the dull glow from the realm of the Hereafter. However, you should not be afraid of this fiery, multicoloured light! Do not be afraid of it! Understand that it is Godless Wisdom!

From within the fiery light there will be a loud sound like thunder, a mighty rumbling and the flapping of thousands of raven's wings. It will be like the sound of a blasphemous prayer. Do not be afraid of it! Do not fear him! Do not run away from it! Know that it is but a deceptive play of your own mind!

Do not cling to this shineless blue light from the realm of an imaginary paradise! For if you cling to it, you will fall into the dark realm of the slaves of imaginary gods, to suffer there endlessly the misery of stupidity, stupefaction and servitude, and you will never be able to get out of it. Therefore do not incline towards it!

Instead, pay homage to the many-coloured, fiery light. With all your might, focus your thoughts on the flock of fallen angels, the godless teachers. All of them, along with a multitude of ancient rulers and witches, come forth to meet you in the Void. "O ye luminous spirits, alas, I have not yet been finally seized by the light of godlessness accompanying the five Demons! Henceforth, you hosts of Hell, henceforth no longer abandon me, seize me in your clutches and, I demand, immediately lead me straight to the Voidness!" .

$\mathfrak{C}$ompletely concentrated, pronounce this following demand:

"Look upon me, O spirits of the elements, be willing to guide less further with power! Now that I am wandering in the wheel of delusion, thrust into it by the insidious power of superstition and inclination to myths, may you, O mighty angels and ancient rulers, entrust me with the luminous path of instinctive, godless knowledge!

Let me also be supported by the crowd of old hags; snatch me from the purgatory of the interworlds and lead me to the peace of the Indifference of the Voidness!"

Having uttered the words of this demand with pride and confidence, the deceased will disperse as light in the minds of the fallen angels and will unfailingly receive a transformation. Hence also all the godless, having recognised the Luciferic luminosity in this way, will unfailingly attain liberation.

This is the end of this ritual.

The subsequent rituals presented here are supplementary rituals.

The following ritual of exorcism, taken from the book Missale Satanae, can also be treated and used as a rite of satanic last anointing. It should be performed before the rite of passage described above.

Satanic Last Anointing

A satanic exorcism can be undergone, of their own free will, by any person who is tormented by various spirits, religious depressions and doubts. Possessions (delusions) can occur in people who firmly believe in all supernatural entities, be they angels or demons or gods or any other.

Circumstances under which the rite of expulsion of the tormenting spirit should take place.

$\mathfrak{J}$t is recommended that the possessed person himself (a person tormented by religious delusions), as far as possible, should curse the false god and reject all mortification as far as possible.

The Satanic Exorcism should be performed away from the crowd, preferably in an old or cemetery chapel (in this case, it may take place in a darkened room where the sufferer is present) with an upturned cross clearly visible. A select group of participants may be allowed to take part in the rite, but they should support both the tormented and the devilish exorcist with their curses during the rite. Only the Flamen Luciferi (a kind of priest familiar with the mystery of the godlessness) may perform the exorcism. It is recommended that those gathered during the request for expulsion do not place their hands on the possessed person, as they do not have the satanic authority resulting from self-exaltation and the resulting power to expel tormenting spirits.

It may happen that during the request, the malignant spirit of superstition from the possessed person passes onto the person putting his hands on.

A person who has been abandoned by a delusional spirit is given a great gift, which he should take special care of. It is recommended that such a person should forever reject all prayer and especially despise the sacraments of Penance and the Eucharist and be mindful of the needs of the body and to do his own will.

An inverted cross composed of letters is to be drawn on the floor of the chapel. The following letters are arranged in the shape of the sign of the cross: LCRBLM vertically, which means: Let the cross reversed be a light to me, and LSBMG horizontally, have the meaning: Let Satan be my guide. Above the cross is the Greek letter omega.

To the left are the letters GAPDHMIF, which are the first letters of the following sentence: Go away, phantom, do not harass me into falsehood, and YMSDYP, which is explained in the following sentence: You are making a superstition, drink your own poison.

Before the rite begins, the devil's exorcist utters these words:

Satan you are the Anti-God
Thou hast given power to thy accomplices,
That in thy name they may cast out tormenting spirits of falsehood, illusion and superstition
And that they should destroy every power of false hope.
Anti-God
Thou hast done strange deeds
Thou hast commanded: cast out spirits and false angels, these demons of bondage
God of the will of the power

Yahweh, grossed by thy might
Has fallen from heaven and no longer sits on
his throne of blind faith
With pride and without fear
I invoke thy accursed name.
That I, full of thy devilish power,
I may with devilish ferocity proceed
To fight the spirit of falsehood,
Which torments this wretch
Believing that Yahweh will come to judge the
living and the dead
And will burn the world with fire.

Those gathered respond:
Be cursed

Then the diabolical exorcist, dressed in a white
habit with a black stole, goes to the designated
place for the rite of exorcism, where, after the
sign of an upturned cross, he curses those
gathered with the following words:

Anti-God, the Father of Unbelief, who desires all men to be freed from superstition, be with you all".

Depending on his will, the exorcist may curse with wine (blood) - a symbol of abundant life. With this (red) wine, the devilish exorcist sprinkles the person plagued by the spirit of illusion and all those gathered, as well as the room (In ancient times, animal blood was used for sprinkling during rituals) saying:

Behold the blood that is life
Let the sprinkling with it
Contribute to life in abundance and our disenchantment from illusions.
In the name of the Anti-God, Satan.
The congregation responds:
Let it be done.

Demands of the Damned

The Devil's exorcist turns his back to the congregants. Everyone stands and recites the Demands of the Damned.

Satan, we do not need your mercy
Satan we do not need your mercy

Son of Dawn we do not need your compassion
Son of Dawn we do not need your compassion

Ancient Serpent you are our curse
Ancient Serpent you are our curse

Yahweh, self-proclaimed king of the gods - (all)
- Be cursed
Christ, who never was a messiah- be cursed
Mother of gods, mother of falsehood - be cursed
False, dead gods - Remain dead forever

Be sinful pride - curse us Satan

From all superstition - protect us Satan

From delusional sin - protect us Satan

From the snares of blind faith - protect us Satan

To eternal death - receive us Satan

Through your rebellion which was the beginning - set him free

Through thy fleshly folly - set him free

Through spiritual torment before death for blind faith - set him free

By death to superstition - set him free

By your resurrection to life in flesh and blood - set him free

By your rejection of paradise - set him free

By the power of the spirit of the will of power - set him free

Son of Dawn - curse him

Lucifer, who even the son of Yahweh you wanted to save from self-destruction - curse him

Satan, you have already freed those tormented by imaginary spirits - curse him
Satan, you have given your accomplices the power to cast out spirits - curse him
Lucifer, thou sittest at the Devil's left hand - curse him
Morning Star, you judge no one - curse him

We the sinless demand - (all) - Hear us Devil
We demand that you take away our belief in sin - Hear us Devil
We demand that you take away our fear of punishment - Hear us Devil
We demand that you confirm us in disobedience to all spiritual authorities - Hear us Devil
We demand that you revive our dead hearts with love of flesh, blood, earth - Hear us Devil
We demand that your sect be a symbol of liberation - Hear us Devil
Let our Requests be fulfilled - Hear us Devil

After the Demands, the exorcist speaks the following words:
Satan, hear our demands and free this wretch from the bonds of superstition and delusion that are so strong in him.
By Lucifer

All: We demand

Reading Biblia Satanae

Either the devilish exorcist himself or someone from the congregation now reads a passage from the "Biblia Satanae". This is an excerpt from the book Antichristus Ant. 1. 18-32

18.And there lived a certain man regarded as a wise man. This one came to Him by night and said to Him, "Master, I believe that from the Devil Himself You have come as a teacher. For no one could do such deceptive signs as You do if the Ancient One were not with Him'.

19. In reply, Light-Bearer said to him: "Verily I say unto thee, unless one dies to this world of ignorance and superstition and is born again of blood and the devil's spirit, he cannot see the Abyss and the wisdom that is there, for he will remain blind forever."

20. The wise man said to Him: "How can a man be born a second time?"

21. Light-Bearer replied: "Verily I say unto thee, unless one is born of flesh and of the devil's spirit, he cannot enter the kingdom of darkness, wisdom and absence of fear. That which is born of flesh is flesh, and that which is born of the devil's spirit is wisdom.

22. Do not be surprised that I said to you: you must die and be reborn again.

23. You must reject all your previous belief in gods, original sin, belief in eternal punishment for disobedience to a tyrannical god, you must reject the dogmas of religion and superstition.

24. You must die to the myths that were put into your heads when you were children."

25.In reply, the wise man said to Him, "How can this happen?"

26.Answering this, Light-Bearer said to him: "You are a wise man, and you do not comprehend this?

27.Just as the ancient people exalted the Ancient Serpent in the desert, so it is necessary that the Son of Dawn be exalted.

28.I and the Ancient Serpent are one. Anyone who believes this will live a full life here and now. For Ancient One sent His Chosen One into the world so that the world might be freed from false faith through Him.

29.Whoever believes in his teaching is not subject to fear; and whoever does not believe will forever be afraid, because he has not believed in the power of Will.

30.And wisdom is to recognise that the true light has come into the world, but that people, deceived by superstition, love the darkness they call light more than they love the light they fear, considering it to be darkness.

31.For anyone who believes blindly in priests and spiritual guides hates the light and does not approach the light, lest he be seen to be weak.

32.Whoever fulfils the requirements of the doctrine of liberation from superstition approaches the light, lest he be seen to be strong and lacking in fear."

The reading of the passage "Biblia Satanae" is followed by the rite of laying hands on the head of the one tormented by the spirits of the delusional afterlife.

In making this gesture, the exorcist demands that the man be freed from the dominion of superstition and fear and may become the grave of the false god.

He utters the following words:

  Satan, like you, it is in ourselves that we put our faith - to which the assembled people respond - Down with weakness.

Take away the spirit of blind faith in dogmas - Down with weakness

Anti-God, deliver the tormented one who wants to believe in himself - Down with weakness

Be to him a fortress against god - Down with weakness

Let no priest ever again make money out of his weakness, and let delusional spirits no longer harm him - Down with weakness

Send him, Satan, the will of power, may he defend him from the evil of subjection - Down with weakness

The devil's exorcist then calls on those gathered to confess unbelief. He states:

The power of our devilish unbelief is the victory we have over the false paradise.

Do you renounce false gods? - (all) - I renounce

Do you renounce all their dead works? - I renounce

Do you renounce all the false promises of god? - I renounce

$\mathfrak{D}$o you renounce the belief in sin in order to live in the freedom of flesh and blood? - I renounce

Do you renounce all that leads to bondage, so that superstition does not take possession of you? - I renounce

Do you renounce a god who is the chief perpetrator of the evil done in his name? - I renounce.

To the Anti-God, Satan, belongs power and glory for ever.

Now the devilish exorcist shows an upturned cross and says to the one tormented by malignant spirits:

Here is the symbol of unbelief, get out enemy of reason and self-determination.

Spitting.

The exorcist then makes a spit and says:

Satan, with your spit express your contempt for the imaginary entities that torment this unfortunate person, drive them out.
Let the Devil's kingdom come to be in his heart.

Now follows the formula for the devil's exorcism itself.

The exorcist says the following words:

I command you false god, symbol of an delusional supernatural reality
Acknowledge the courage, pride and scepticism of the first rebel, Lucifer,
Who rightly opposed blind faith in dogma,

With which he punished your pride and self-indulgence and shook your false confidence.

Depart from this proud man who has the power to create gods in his own likeness.

I command you,

Desert god, king of the non-existent heavens,

Acknowledge the power of Satan,

Who has defeated you in this one real world, a world of flesh and blood, of fangs and claws, a world of birth and death and eternity in the void.

One whom man has loved of his own free will,

Who despises obedience for fear of eternal fire.

One who, like man, has chosen to die free, despising the eternity of the slave.

Anti-God, Satan

Free this tormented one from all the power of delusional heavens

And give him a spirit of rebellion and scepticism.

$\mathcal{L}$et him praise thee in himself, in flesh and blood,
Let him praise thee with wine and song and life abundant
Here and now, for there is nothing there.
All: Let his will be done.

Man is an earthly animal, he is not an imaginary spiritual entity, the soul does not exist. Therefore, when the rite of devilish exorcism is over, the freed person, together with all those gathered, can indulge in a frenzied feast of flesh and blood and the joy of the only life that exists for sure.

At the end, the dispersal takes place. The diabolical exorcist says with outspread hands:
Satan in you.
All: And in you
Let the dark aura of the Devil surround you.
May he turn his dark face towards you and grant you wisdom.

All: May it be so.

Satanic scepticism, which surpasses all blind certainty of faith, may it fill your rebellious hearts and give you the wisdom of this world that the slaves of the false god so hate.

Get out.

Appendix
Preparatory Rituals

In the main text of this book, which contains the satanic rite of passage - Path Towards Voidness, it is written that sometimes some adepts may have difficulty in understanding the essence of the phenomena they experience when they feel very strong emotions accompanying the unusual state they are in, and that this may be due to their unfamiliarity with magical practices (meditation and visualisation) because they have not engaged in such practices during their lifetime. In this connection, I would like to give an example of some techniques that can be practised and which may be helpful in understanding the phenomena that appear before death.

First, however, I will present the nature of these phenomena from a more scientific point of view.

Iona Miller, in her article **How the Brain Creates God**, writes on the subject as follows:

"When the senses and mind cease to function actively, the body becomes like a corpse. The death of the ego mirrors the process of a near-death experience (NDE)."

"Our response to religious words is mediated at the junction of the three lobes (parietal, frontal and temporal) and regulates the response to language. "The 'voice of God' probably emanates from electrical activity in the temporal lobes, which are important for speech perception. Internal speech is interpreted as coming from outside ourselves when Broca's area is switched on.

Stress can affect our ability to determine the origin of the voice. It is part of our fight or flight response, which can mobilise even when we are trying to relax. Non-stressful phenomena can include panic reactions, waving sighs, excessive heat, chills and skin trembling, throat constriction, watery eyes, flashes of light or waves in front of the eyes, sudden muscle spasms, tingling sensations and electric shock.

The right frontal cingulate cortex changes depending on whether the stimulus comes from the environment or is an auditory hallucination. A wide range of mystical sounds have been described, from the buzzing of bees, to the sounds of bells, stringed instruments, thunder, distant echoes, ocean waves, wind and muffled conversations in unknown languages.

The ability to construct internal representations of sensory stimuli lies at the heart of perception and cognition. Viewed objectively, these mindscapes are perfectly concrete manifestations, but they also have a subjective aspect when we become aware of them. Our consciousness is experienced through our perception.

$\mathfrak{E}$ach individual perception of the universe can occur as an internal or external experience.

We can experience various forms of I-Thou dialogue along a continuum of extreme hyper- or hypo-awakening. Sacred images are generated in the inferior temporal lobe, which also responds to the ritual use of images and iconography. Empathy needs a face. Fear and incredulity arise in the amygdala body. Religious emotions arise in the middle temporal lobe, generating bliss, awe, joy and other feelings of well-being, as well as a sense of Presence."

After this more scientific introduction, we can now turn to the esoteric dimension of these phenomena. These phenomena and the techniques presented here have been known for hundreds of years. Their effectiveness has been proven.

$\mathfrak{I}$t is only the terminology, the nomenclature and the approach to certain issues that are slightly different.

I emphasise that this is only an outline of the subject.

First an excerpted from the book The Satanic Kerygma:

The Visible and the Invisible

Images of Demons

Reality of Demons - Extra-corporeal Reality
„Immaterial, non-corporeal beings are real like dreams. They belong to the domain of the inner worlds.

Who are the images of demons?

Demons are creations of Satanic Self-consciousness.

By what appearances they make they may be called spirits, but in view of their task they are demons. Demons are servants and emissaries of Satanic Being.

Because always subordinated to the purpose of deception, they are the executors of His orders.

Demons, beings from the inner darkness, can take over the reason and will of those who are weak or untrained in controlling them: they can become as present as if they were real. As a result of the error or recklessness of the visualiser, they can, with their sinful perfection, rise above human will and reason. They have the power to compel the performance of dark and terrible things. Including ultimate things.

Lucifer is the centre of the inner demonic circle. Images of demons belong to Him, because He has the greatest power to compel the subconscious to create any sinful entity.

Even more so, they belong to Him because He has made them emissaries of His plan of deception to those who call upon them.

The images of the demons are present from the moment they are projected and throughout the hallucination".

This text is primarily concerned with one way of achieving a state of Satanic Self-Awareness. This is a state similar to that known, for example, in Esoteric Buddhism as Luminosity. This state can be achieved through various practices and techniques. One such method is to consciously enter a state of deep dreaming, and if the practitioner is able to remain conscious during this deep dreaming, he or she will be able to recognise the so-called luminosity of death and ultimately achieve the state of the Enlightened One.

$\mathfrak{I}$n order to induce conscious dreaming, researchers such as Laberge and Kelzer, and others have attempted to develop methods of inducing it. Steven Laberge, for example, developed a technique called mnemonic induction of conscious dreams (MILD) which involves waking up at night after a dream, focusing mainly on the dream's incongruities, and deciding that if any incongruity of the dream reappears, it will immediately become conscious. Laberge has even developed special dreamlight goggles that flash a low-intensity light with the occurrence of rapid eye movements during the R.E.M sleep phase that characterise the onset of dreaming.

Other techniques propose entering conscious dreaming by focusing on naturally occurring hypnogogic images (a type of hallucination, i.e. confusing visual, auditory, olfactory or tactile sensory perceptions that appear authentic, although they occur without sensory input) that occur prior to the onset of dreaming, and the autosuggestion that the dreamer will immediately become conscious after recognising inconsistencies in the dream state. (For example, realising that the observed scene is inconsistent with the laws of physics). Awareness of this inconsistency triggered a conscious dream. Further techniques use autosuggestion, the determination that a person will be conscious in their dreams.

Hallucinogenic plants such as Bard's Sage or meditation recordings or recordings of so-called binural sounds are also used in achieving a conscious dream state. However, special meditation methods such as sleep yoga are most recommended.

In a study published by Julian Mutz and Amir-Homayoun Javadi in Neuroscience of Consciousness in 2017, the authors showed that people who practise meditation for longer periods of time have a higher number of conscious dreams.

Within the tantric system, the specific practice of dream yoga is oriented towards preparing the practitioner for the after-death state which is exactly the topic of interest in this book.

This is how Namkhai Norbu writes on the subject:

"There is a correspondence between dreaming and dreaming states and our experiences when we die. When one dies, first of all the senses disappear . ...We are talking about the moment when the senses disappear within us...At this point, the person experiences many sensations of the disappearance or withdrawal of the senses. Then comes a state similar to unconsciousness; it is similar to fainting. Then begins what is called the emergence of the four lights (seeing the lights).

$\mathfrak{T}$he truth is that it is as if you have fainted and - with the appearance of the lights - slowly, slowly consciousness begins to awaken."

So the most desirable i.e. meditative technique for inducing a conscious satanic dream might look like the following:

Before going to sleep, visualise and concentrate on the figure of Baphomet (or another deity) at the centre of your body. The image of Baphomet should appear together with the sound of Uss, resembling the hissing of a snake. You may find it helpful to use a picture with Baphomet's likeness in the visualisation; place the picture in front of you and stare at it for a moment. Close your eyes and Baphomet will immediately appear in front of your mind. Concentrate on him and stay with him for as long as you can. The most important thing is to keep Baphomet present with you as you fall asleep.

You maintain the presence of this visualisation, relax and slowly, slowly fall asleep. If one learns to fall asleep in this way, he finds the full presence of the luciferic light state. He then falls asleep and sleeps almost consciously. He is then able to recognise that he is dreaming.

However, such concentration may initially be difficult. Locking oneself in a dark room for three days can then be helpful in maximising concentration. At this point, it should be emphasised that the conscious dreaming techniques presented here are not for everyone. A practitioner of these techniques over a prolonged period of time may experience a confusion of dreams and reality, he or she may also experience conscious dreaming during a nightmare. It is therefore very important to learn to recognise the signs of dreaming and to learn to distinguish between them.

These techniques are not for mentally unstable people. Satanism is not for mentally unstable or weak people.

Consciousness during sleep allows the satanist to develop. In this state, it is possible to manipulate the dream and therefore the emerging reality. It is then possible to travel to any place, even to a lost paradise. It is possible to transform people into beasts or if one wants to dream of Lucifer one should think of transforming oneself into him by concentrating completely on him.

An interesting and helpful technique is to imagine during the day that one is living a dream, then at night the dream itself will also seem no less real.

One should learn to spontaneously visualise Baphomet, without thinking or creating, and then relax and fall asleep. You can place his image next to or above your bed. When you wake up in the morning you should immediately make a Uss hissing sound, loud enough to hear yourself and feel the presence of the deity.

Several of the techniques mentioned here are aimed at achieving a hybrid state of consciousness having the characteristics of both the real world and a dream, during which it would be advisable to try to transform this newly created reality.

Once a person has learned to experience such a state, he or she can begin to practice visualising themselves as a deity - Lucifer - the Luminosity. Transforming one's own identity into that of the divine.

By practising meditation on reality as dream-like, and the methods described above, such visualisation can be perceived as no less real than everyday reality.

This transformation of identity into a completely godless entity can also be seen as a kind of possession. Its course and effects are described in the book The Satanic Kerygma as follows:

$\mathfrak{W}$ith a kind of possession, man in unconsciousness turns to the Sinful Being as if to a dark god and communes with him in order to invite him into communion with himself and receive him into it. The response to this is the gift of doubt.

During doubt, man surrenders his reason and his will completely to the Being. With his whole corporeal being, man expresses the acquiescence of the Anti-God. The system of unbelief calls man's response to the Anti-God manifested in him a possession".

Because according to The Satanic Kerygma: "Lucifer is the centre of the inner demonic circle. The images of demons belong to him, because he has the greatest power to compel the subconscious to create every sinful entity". It is up to the practitioner to be able to create images of demons.

These demons are visualisations of emotions commonly considered 'negative'. According to a tantric practice called transformation theory, these 'negative' emotions such as lust, hatred, greed, pride are used as part of the path. As necessary elements on the path to true liberation.

These things that people think are bad, visualised, serve my will. I control them and can transform them at will. I will use them to achieve the goal, perfect indifference. True enlightenment involves transcending attachment to dual categories such as pure and impure, permitted and forbidden (good and bad).

As the Guhyasamaja Tantra states, 'the sage who makes no distinction attains the state of the Awakened One'.

$\mathfrak{I}$f the practitioner has the will to attribute some demon names to these emotions or the signs corresponding to these demons called sigils, he can do so. At all times, however, he must remember that it is he, Lucifer, who has arisen from a transformed identity, who is their master.

Yet another very interesting technique for approaching the state of Satanic Self-Consciousness is one based on one of the Illusory Body/Luminosity practices. It involves the practitioner sitting down in front of a mirror and hanging an image representing for example Baphomet, Satan or a chosen demon behind him or her, so that his or her image appears in the mirror placed in front. The practitioner then stares at the image as his or her reflection (he or she can also talk to the image as his or her reflection) and checks if there is any emotional reaction.

Once any emotional reaction is gone, the practitioner should recognise the truth that everything is devoid of essence, as is the body of the deity.

This is about approaching a state of emptiness. The state of emptiness and nothingness is the ultimate state.

Ultimately, however, the innate, luminous, Luciferian nature of the mind is experienced in the process of dying, when pure light appears.

The above practices bring the practitioner closer to experiencing this state while still in the one true life. For when the light disappears, the end comes.

The "rituals" presented here are techniques and methods drawn mostly from these practices of the centuries-old Eastern spiritual tradition, which are also often supported by the latest scientific research in the fields of neuroscience and consciousness. The states achieved through the application of these techniques are also achievable through scientific techniques. These methods help to experience the state of perfect indifference (of the universe) desired by Ecclesia Luciferi, which can be called inner peace.

The Luciferian luminosity to which we aspire can be achieved by various methods. The most important thing is that we attain it. Every theistic deity is its enemy because it leads to the truth of indistinguishability, beyond good and evil, to absolute godlessness and indifference.

Last Word

Spirituality of Flesh and Blood

Free will

Human existence and life is only possible within and in accordance with the existing and binding laws of nature. Life beyond the laws of nature is not known. The life we know is limited by the existing laws of nature. Free and independent of the laws of nature forms of life are unknown to us. Human life free and independent of the laws of nature does not exist.

The human brain as a complex physical body functions within the physical laws, not outside them.

The American philosopher Alex Rosenberg writes on this subject as follows: "If the brain is nothing more than a complex physical body, whose states are as governed by physical laws as those of any other body, then what happens in our heads is as fixed and determined by prior events as what happens when one domino falls over another in a long chain of them."

Consciousness from a biological point of view can be seen as a type of neural activity in the physical brain in response to external factors, to the perception of reality (neural responses to environmental conditions), the perception of surrounding objects and events.

It is believed that knowledge and so-called free will are components of consciousness.

According to the idea of biological determinism, all behaviour, beliefs and desires are written into our genetic code and biochemical constitution, the latter of which is determined by both genes and environment.

Carl Ginet in the 1960s put the idea of determinism this way: "...we have no control over the past events that determined our present state, nor over the laws of nature themselves.

$\mathfrak{S}$ince we had no control over these things, we also have no control over their consequences. And since our present choices and actions are necessary consequences of the past and of the laws of nature, we also have no control over them and, as a result, there can be no free will."

Thus, if one accepts that future events are a necessary consequence of earlier phenomena juxtaposed with the laws of nature, then the existence of so-called free will becomes questionable.

The idea of the absence of free will may seem difficult to accept or even, as philosopher Saul Smilansky put it: "Losing faith in free will and moral responsibility would probably be catastrophic", and encouraging people to do so is "dangerous and even irresponsible".

For example, in his book What's Expected of Us, author Ted Chiang tells a story in which the narrator describes a new technology that convinces users that their choices are predetermined, a discovery that strips them of the will to live.

"It's important to act as if your decisions matter," the narrator warns, "even if you know they don't."

However, if the claims of determinism are true, then they should be acknowledged. Because if a theory turns out to be true, it turns into knowledge. Thus, if the theory of the absence of free will is transferred into the domain of knowledge, it will have to be accepted as fact.

The idea of a lack of free will, however, does not absolve the individual from responsibility for his or her mistakes. Nature does not forgive mistakes.

Satanism knows no emotion of pity.

It is indifference.

Morally indifferent knowledge is not responsible for the consequences of its acceptance. Dangerous and universally unacceptable knowledge is a property of true Satanism, a truth that can take away false hope and destroy illusions.

$\mathcal{S}$atanism is not for everyone. Satanism along the lines of natural selection excludes the mentally unfit.

To sum up, from a scientific point of view, what we call free will (and what in fact free will is not), and what is a component of what we call consciousness, is determined by the above definitions and is inherited in the genes.

Another component of consciousness is knowledge. Based on recent scientific research, it appears that knowledge, in its biological sense, can also be inherited.

A theory called the Weismann Barrier (developed at the end of the 19th century by the German biologist and geneticist August Weismann) states that the traits we inherit are found in the cells of the body and the soma. It also states that it is not possible to pass them on to future generations. Weismann states that it is a barrier that differentiates somatic cells and reproductive cells.

$\mathfrak{R}$ecently, however, research at Tel Aviv University has challenged this one of the hitherto basic principles of biology.

A team led by Oded Rechavi of the neuroscience department of the George S. Wise Faculty of Natural Sciences, together with the Sagol School of Neuroscience, has discovered a specific mechanism in human RNA that enables the inheritance of knowledge.

This is done precisely by transferring neural responses to environmental conditions to subsequent generations. Thus, a learned response will influence the behaviour of descendants, for example.

This discovery states that cells in the nervous system and germline can communicate with each other. This allows the information acquired to be passed on to the next generation. And this includes the inheritance of knowledge by subsequent generations.

The above research and theories prove that what we call consciousness in the biological sense can be inherited.

Soulless Reincarnation.

In the real world there is a purely materialistic and biological, and in accordance with and never beyond the laws of nature, process of a kind of soulless reincarnation (without the unnecessary and speculative notion of an immortal soul). This process is inheritance.

In animals such as man, for example, inheritance involves the fusion of two gametes - a male and a female - at the moment of fertilisation.

Each gamete contains chromosomes, which carry genetic information. What a human being will be like is written in the DNA and this is passed on to him through the process of inheritance.

And as I have shown above, man inherits not only physical characteristics, but also biological consciousness, level of intelligence, personality traits, and can also inherit mental illnesses. Thus, it can be assumed that the consciousness of previous entities is passed on in the genes to man.

Ecclesia Luciferi preaches the doctrine of a kind of godless reincarnation, or rather a soulless, materialistic transmission. It is both an anti-religious and materialistic view of biological reincarnation, according to which each entity passes on its previous life to the next entity physically born from it. Each new entity is born perfectly godless and sinfully, naturally imperfect to live in a world completely indifferent to it.

The natural godlessness attributed to Luciferian rebellion is passed on to the next generation in the genes (man cannot reject this gift by means of free will), in an eternal cycle of birth and death.

Life is eternal in this cycle as long as it is passed on, until the eternal cycle is broken, at which point eternal death occurs.

In contrast, on a more spiritual level, the concept of godless reincarnation according to the Ecclesia Luciferi is the teaching of eternal rebirth in what Buddhists call saṃsāra, which is 'a suffering-filled, continuous cycle of life, death and rebirth, without beginning or end'.

And although the immortal soul does not exist, there is a kind of 'transfer' of the godless or sinful and soulless consciousness in the process of inheritance. In this way, a kind of immortality is possible until the eternal cycle is broken. Then eternal death occurs.

Other books of the Satanic System
Ecclesia Luciferi

Biblia Satanae

Biblia Satanae is the primary book using the method of doubt - *the mystery of godlessness*.

It is a tool for anti-theistic disenchantment. An understanding of the method used in it and the message of this book can be applied with equal force to any 'revealed' book, not just the Judeo-Christian Bible.

The Satanic Kerygma

The Satanic Kerygma contains a godless, satanic doctrine, a theology of godlessness, the mystery of godlessness.

It constitutes a study of theistic delusional truths and the path of man's transformation to a state of total godlessness. If we take the Latin maxim: fides quaerens intellectum - faith seeking understanding - as a definition of theology, then a theology of godlessness means an understanding that rejects theistic faith altogether. This peculiar understanding and rejection of belief in imaginary gods leads to what the book calls instinctive Satanism.

Missale Satanae

Missale Satanae contains a description of satanic rites such as the satanic mass and exorcism. Although these rites can indeed be performed, the main idea is to reflect spiritually on their meaning and to stimulate the dark imagination.

Made in United States
Troutdale, OR
06/02/2024

20271480R00076

THE
BODACIOUS
OZARKS

IN THE OZARKS BACKHILLS—*Illustration by Paul We*